CONTENTS

INTRODUCTION

Electricity accounts for 25% of the fuel used in British agriculture. It makes a major contribution to UK food production in crop drying and storage, livestock production and commercial horticulture. It has more applications in UK agriculture than anywhere else in the world and, used safely, is a powerful aid to farming.

Like livestock, chemicals or tractors, electricity is perfectly safe if treated with care and respect. However, its misuse or poor maintenance can lead to accidents, sometimes fatal, as well as damage to property.

Few staff have had training on the electrical equipment they use everyday. So the purpose of this booklet is to highlight hazards which arise from bad practice and to provide practical guidelines on the safe use of electricity on the farm and in horticulture. These basic principles have been brought together with the help of a number of interested organisations.

Accidents don't just happen, they are caused mainly by lack of care or knowledge. We hope that, through the advice in this booklet, the number of electrical accidents will be reduced.

The booklet will help you decide which aspects of the selection, installation, operation and maintenance of the electrical system are best left to your electrical contractor and will help you brief him. It will also help you undertake basic electrical tasks safely.

ELECTRICITY DOSSIER

Those who work on a farm should know where the electrical cables are, overhead, underground or installed within the farm buildings. The Electricity Companies can help provide this information. It is strongly recommended that an 'Electricity Dossier' be created for each farm. It should contain the maps and diagrams showing the whole electrical system and be kept up-to-date. The plans should show the positions of all meters, switches, sockets, fuses, MCBs, RCDs and all permanently connected equipment. The dossier should also contain the reports and certificates of all inspections and records of all work done on the system.

It is also a good idea to keep handy a note of any emergency phone numbers for supply faults, accidents and for any electrical repairs.

(M)636.371E

GENERAL DO'S AND DON'TS

To use electricity safely, follow the do's and don'ts listed below. They highlight the principles which are dealt with more fully in the following chapters.

DO...

▲ DO... employ a competent electrical contractor experienced in farm wiring and approved by the NICEIC (see page 5) to carry out all work on the electrical system including: connections, disconnections, new and extended wiring, repairs and maintenance.

▲ DO... have the electrical system regularly inspected and maintained by a competent electrical contractor, this is required by law, and obtain certificates of these inspections.

▲ DO... ensure that electrical installations comply with the current IEE Wiring Regulations (see page 5).

▲ DO... contact a competent electrical contractor when in any doubt about the safety of electrical equipment or the installation.

▲ DO... use only electrical equipment and accessories designed to cope with the prevailing conditions, eg that conform to BS 4343 and IP44 or higher specifications.

▲ DO... use correct waterproof plugs, sockets and switches in damp or wet areas or where hosing or cleaning takes place.

▲ DO... handle switches and apparatus with dry hands, especially in milking parlours and other wet situations.

▲ DO... cover electrical equipment and switches with waterproof sheeting when hosing or steam cleaning.

▲ DO... ensure that everyone involved in the use of electricity is fully informed of these safety requirements.

▲ DO... arrange for replacement or repair of damaged wiring or accessories.

▲ DO... keep motors, ventilating fans and airways free of dust and airborne debris.

▲ DO... check thermostat settings frequently.

▲ DO... beware of the dangers from overhead lines and underground cables.

▲ DO... take care when moving long objects near overhead lines, when digging holes and every time you use portable or transportable equipment.

▲ DO... test RCDs (residual current devices) and visually examine the associated earth wire (if fitted), especially after storms and lightning.

▲ DO...use a properly constructed (purpose made) extension lead if extra cable length is needed.

▲ DO... ensure that the extension lead is completely uncoiled from its drum before it is used.

▲ DO... ensure electrical connections are properly made with plugs and sockets and that terminal screws are fully tightened and checked regularly.

▲ DO... make sure that the cable grips in plugs are used and correctly applied, ie securely tightened on to the cable sheath.

▲ DO... switch off and unplug portable electrical equipment before maintenance or repairs are undertaken.

▲ DO... check the condition of electric tools and their cables before use, and store them in a clean dry place.

DON'T...

▲ DON'T... attempt to extend or modify existing wiring installations, this is a job for a competent electrical contractor.

▲ DON'T... connect or use faulty equipment or circuits: if in any doubt, switch off and call in an electrician; remember electric shocks can be fatal.

▲ DON'T... attempt to carry out electrical repairs yourself.

▲ DON'T... overload circuits or cables.

▲ DON'T... use wrong size or 'make-do' fuses.

▲ DON'T... use multiple adaptors.

▲ DON'T... allow long flexible leads to become a permanent part of the system.

▲ DON'T... attempt to adjust the setting of circuit overload devices or make other adjustments within control panels.

▲ DON'T... attempt to connect a portable generator to an electrical system except at a properly designed and installed connection point; this is a job for a competent electrical contractor (see page 23).

▲ DON'T... attempt to connect heating lamps to lighting circuits.

▲ DON'T... use resistance regulators for controlling the speed of fans or for the control of lighting.

WHEN USING PORTABLE OR TRANSPORTABLE EQUIPMENT

▲ DON'T... connect electric tools to lighting circuits.

▲ DON'T... use portable heaters in damp conditions eg in a milking parlour.

▲ DON'T... route trailing leads where they are likely to be damaged.

▲ DON'T... extend cables or flexible leads by means of temporary joints, use purpose designed couplers to BS 4343, IP44 or higher specification.

▲ DON'T... attempt to wire plugs to cables which have non-standard colours; seek advice.

HOUSEKEEPING

▲ DON'T... pile bags of fertilizer or other obstructions close to switches or control panels and so make it difficult to switch off quickly in the event of an emergency.

▲ DON'T... erect buildings, stacks or clamps under or close to overhead lines.

▲ DON'T... move tall machinery under or in the vicinity of overhead lines until the safety clearances have been checked.

▲ DON'T... assume that overhead line conductors which have fallen are dead (see page 27).

REGULATIONS AND THE LAW

The Health and Safety at Work etc. Act 1974 requires that everyone at work has a responsibility not to put themselves or others at risk by their acts and omissions.

Employers, you also have the responsibility to ensure that an electrical system is safe. This means that if you are not qualified yourself to wire or maintain an installation, then you should employ someone who is, to:
(a) advise you on the standard of wiring and equipment you require and
(b) carry out the installation to those standards.

The Electricity at Work Regulations 1989 apply to farms. They place duties on employers, employees and the self-employed in so far as they relate to matters which are within their control.

They require that:
▲ the electrical system is sound and has been properly installed and maintained (the installation standards set out in the IEE Regulations for Electrical Installations are considered acceptable in this respect).

▲ the electrical system means all the electrical equipment which is or may be connected to a common source of electrical energy and includes both the source and the equipment.

▲ persons carrying out electrical work must be competent to do so.

▲ expert advice should be sought in order to establish satisfactory arrangements for inspection and maintenance.

▲ electrical safety be included in the general safety arrangements that relate to the organisation, including routine safety checks.

*Regional Electricity Companies are approved NICEIC electrical contractors

NB No farmer or worker should ever attempt to work on live equipment.

There are stringent regulations that cover working on live equipment that only a competent electrical contractor could comply with.

In this country the recognised standards of safety and good practice are those set out in the IEE Wiring Regulations (*Regulations for Electrical Installations* published by the Institution of Electrical Engineers).

Always employ an electrical contractor listed by the National Inspection Council for Electrical Installation Contracting (NICEIC) (referred to as an Approved Electrical Contractor)*.

You are strongly recommended to employ such a firm, since its standard of work is subject to periodic checks by NICEIC inspectors. While the contractor can recommend suitable cables, fittings and conduit for your farm, it is as well to know that there are appropriate British Standards or Codes of Practice for particular farming situations.

These are listed in Appendix 2. You should also be aware that the IEE Wiring Regulations make reference to a large number of British Standards which should be complied with.

Because of the adverse conditions in farming and horticulture and the high susceptibility of farm animals to electric shock, the IEE Wiring Regulations set out certain regulations which apply specifically to these premises.

When a wiring installation has been completed you should obtain a document signed by the contractor certifying that it has been installed in accordance with the IEE Wiring Regulations.

SAFETY PRACTICES

The Electricity at Work Regulations require that the electrical system be constructed and maintained so as to prevent danger. Nor should anyone work in such a way as to give rise to danger. For example if an area is damp, wet or subject to hosing and cleaning then the electrical system must be proof against these conditions.

The following precautions can help maintain safety around the farm:

▲ motors and their controls should be kept clear of obstructions.

▲ the electrical system should be protected against damage from people, animals, machines and vehicles.

▲ warning labels and signs should be used to draw attention to the presence of the electric installation and its accessories.

▲ test RCDs every time before using equipment connected to them.

▲ look at equipment to check that it is dry before use.

▲ operate electrical switches with dry hands.

▲ only waterproof extension cables should be used in wet conditions.

▲ keep all other extension cables in the dry.

▲ if there is any doubt that fixed electric

Splashproof lightswitch

Use waterproof connectors in wet conditions

equipment and switches are not fully protected, cover and secure them with waterproof sheeting before cleaning with a hose or steam cleaners.

▲ avoid directing hoses at the electrical system or equipment.

Preventive maintenance of the electrical system is essential and is required under the Electricity at Work Regulations. Regular inspection is a key part of any maintenance programme.*

You should arrange for an approved electrical contractor to check the system regularly. Repairs may be necessary because of the harsh environment of an agricultural or horticultural holding. The frequency of inspections will depend on the extent of repairs and the use that the system is subjected to.

Keep a check on damage to insulation, switches, socket outlets and other fittings. Remember, an exposed terminal may be lethal. Any damage to electrical equipment should be regarded as an emergency to be repaired without delay. Keep an eye on earth leads and if you find any damaged or disconnected, get an electrician to put them right.

Do not assume that redundant wiring is safe, get an electrician to disconnect and remove it.

*Your local Electricity Company will be pleased to undertake such an inspection and any remedial work

THE ELECTRICAL SYSTEM

Electricity is widely used in milking parlours

This comprises the cables, conduit, main switches, distribution boards, trunking, junction boxes and accessories that contain the current carrying wires from the Electricity Company's meter to the points of use throughout the farm or horticultural holding.

EARTHING

The provision of earthing in an electrical circuit is one of the vital safety measures.

The purpose of earthing is to prevent the non-current carrying metal parts of the system (eg the outside casing) from becoming live in the event of a circuit fault. If a fault occurs in an electrical appliance and its metal parts are not earthed, they may become live.

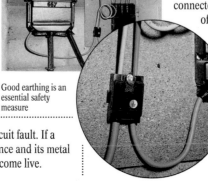

Good earthing is an essential safety measure

Should a person or animal make contact with them it could cause a current to flow through their bodies to earth with possible fatal results.

Wet hands and wet conditions can increase the danger. Wearing rubber boots must not be relied on to provide protection.

If the apparatus is properly connected to an efficient earth of the right size and a fault occurs, the fault current will be safely discharged to earth and the protective devices described next, will disconnect the equipment.

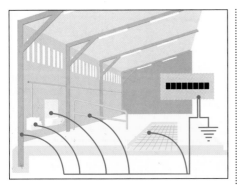

Bond metalwork to earth

SAFETY DEVICES (FUSES AND MINIATURE CIRCUIT BREAKERS)

These devices are used to disconnect an electric circuit automatically if a fault or overload occurs. The most familiar are fuses, but miniature circuit breakers (MCBs) are becoming more widely used.

FUSES

The main function of fuses is to protect against damage due to temperature rise caused by excess current in the fixed installation. A fuse is a small piece of wire in a circuit designed to melt when a certain current passes through it thus limiting the current and breaking the circuit when the limit is exceeded. It is essential to use a fuse of the correct type and rating for the circuit it is intended to protect, and to keep spares to hand. Never increase the size of a circuit fuse, it could lead to a fire. The fuse must always be the weakest link in the circuit.

The provision of adequate earthing is the responsibility of the person owning and using the electrical system, but the method of earthing must be decided by a qualified electrical contractor. It is essential that a contractor should consult the local office of the Electricity Company about the availability of a suitable earth connection. It is dangerous to rely upon metal water pipes to provide an earth path, because of the increasing use of plastic and other non-metallic pipes for carrying water.

Metalwork in farm buildings needs bonding to earth. Protective bonding is a complex subject and should be undertaken by a competent contractor.

Once an earthing system has been installed, it is essential to maintain it in a safe condition. While this can be achieved by a maintenance contract, it is essential to keep an eye open for possible deterioration of the earthing system. If, for example, earth wires are accidentally broken or disconnected they should be replaced immediately. This is particularly important in and around milking parlours.

Rewireable fuses and fuse carriers

A main fuse protects the whole wiring system connected to it. A smaller fuse is used to protect an individual circuit, and a fused plug (of the correct rating) protects the cable to which it is attached. A fuse will not provide direct protection against electric shock or fire (see under Earthing above). An RCD is required.

Fixed equipment, eg motors for mills, dryers or milking plant, should have separate circuits complete with control switches and fuses. These should always be clearly labelled for ease of identification.

Two main types of fuse are in common use:

Rewireable fuses

comprising a 'carrier' made of porcelain or other insulating material, having a terminal at each end, the space between being bridged by a fuse wire of appropriate rating.

Cartridge fuses

in which the wire cannot be replaced. These consist of an insulating tube with metal endcaps and an enclosed fuse element. When a small cartridge fuse 'blows' it cannot usually be detected by visual examination.

Replacing a fuse

Fuses and fuse wire are rated according to their capacity to carry continuous current eg: 3, 5, 13, 15, 30, 45 and 60 amps.

Wire must **never** be fitted to carriers designed for cartridge fuses and on no account must other substitutes be used with either type.

Fuse tester

Should equipment cease to function, the following procedure is recommended.

❶ Disconnect by switching off at a local switch and, if applicable, remove the plug from the socket outlet.

❷ Check the plug for any loose terminal connections and/or damage to cables or equipment.

❸ If a 13 amp plug is involved, the plug fuse may have 'blown'. Check by replacing with a new fuse of correct rating and switch on. Should equipment still not function, switch off and test the fuse in a proprietary fuse tester. (see above)

❹ Turn off relevant main control switch and examine the **circuit** fuse.

❺ Locate and remove any 'blown' fuse wire or cartridge fuse from its carrier.

❻ Replace with the same rated wire (if the rewireable type), or the same type and rating (if the cartridge type).

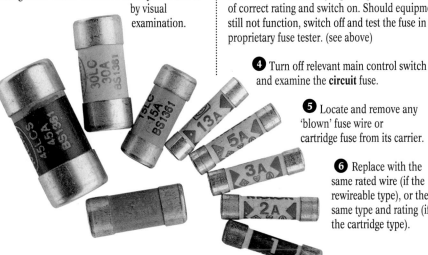
Cartridge fuses

7 With the fuse replaced, close the fusebox and switch on main and equipment switches.

NB If the fuse 'blows' again or the equipment still does not work, call in a competent electrical contractor.

Never attempt to get equipment working by increasing the size or number of strands of fuse wire.

MINIATURE CIRCUIT BREAKERS - MCBS (NOT RCDS)

This protective device consists of a totally enclosed electrical switch. It 'trips out', ie switches off automatically when excess current arises in the circuit. It can be reset manually if there is no persistent fault. The position of the operating lever or push button shows whether the breaker is ON or OFF. When a fault has been cleared, current is restored by operating the lever or button.

Fault checking if a circuit breaker trips

The action to take in the event of a fault causing the breaker to trip is:

1 Switch off and unplug the suspect apparatus at local control (as for 'Fuses').

2 Check for any loose terminal connections and/or damage to cables or equipment.

3 If a 13 amp plug is involved, the plug fuse may have 'blown'. Check by replacing with a new fuse of correct rating and switch on. Should equipment still not function, switch off and test the fuse in a proprietary fuse tester.

4 Re-close the circuit breaker by means of the lever or button. If the switch remains ON, the fault probably lies in the apparatus switched off. The apparatus should then be examined by a competent electrical contractor.

If 'tripping' still occurs, the fault lies elsewhere, and again the electrical contractor should be called in.

RESIDUAL CURRENT DEVICES - RCDS

RCDs provide a backup defence against electric shock or fire to supplement insulation, earthing, enclosure and protective barriers. They are sensitive devices that detect an imbalance in the currents flowing in the live and neutral conductors. This operates a relay and thus isolates the circuit.

RCDs provide a high standard of protection against the effects of earth leakage faults particularly in situations where there are difficulties in obtaining an effective earth connection. The decision to use and install them is a matter for the specialist, and you are advised to accept the recommendations of a competent contractor.

Where an RCD is installed, operating the test button before every use will either give the assurance that the RCD works, or warn, if the supply does not 'trip out', that the RCD needs specialist attention.

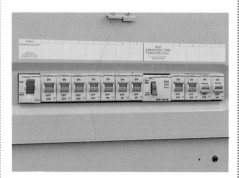

Consumer unit with MCBs built-in

Test RCDs before use

Should other methods fail, RCDs offer additional protection against dangers associated with faulty equipment or wiring. RCDs do not replace overcurrent protection (fuses/MCBs) and earthing but supplement them. RCD protection is recommended for all portable equipment used in the workshop, outdoors or in the wet.

In spite of the advantages of RCDs they occasionally give rise to inconvenience, because of their sensitivity, by tripping out unpredictably. They are in fact doing their job by detecting very small leakage currents. If this 'nuisance tripping' happens frequently then specialist help should be sought.

SOCKET OUTLETS, FLEXIBLE CABLES AND PLUGS

Socket Outlets

Socket outlets, or sockets, are the electrical fittings, usually fixed, to which electricity is brought by cables. They should be installed by a competent contractor. If a socket is required on an extension lead, the best course is to buy a ready-made three core lead. Don't be tempted to make up an extension lead. Never extend any supply by tape joining separate cables together. This is illegal.

On farms, electrical fittings often have to withstand damp, dust or corrosion, and may be subject to cleaning routines involving pressure or steam hosing. Therefore socket outlets should be of robust construction. They should be splashproof (perhaps even hoseproof) and fitted with protective covers to prevent entry of water when the plug is removed. Industrial type sockets outlets made to comply with

Hoseproof and dustproof

BS 4343, fit these requirements.

Socket outlets intended for equipment used outdoors should be protected by an RCD.

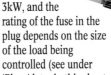

The round pin sockets and wiring of older installations should be replaced because of its age. There may be installed domestic type 13 amp sockets for use with 3 flat pin fused plugs. The 13 amp socket can cope with loads up to 3kW, and the rating of the fuse in the plug depends on the size of the load being controlled (see under 'Plugs' later in this chapter).

RCD protected socket

13 amp sockets and plugs are designed for the ring main wiring system. They may not be suitable for the adverse environmental conditions on the farm.

For any loading in excess of 3kW, special sockets capable of carrying the higher currents are required, and for control of motors in excess of 0.37kW (0.5hp), starters are required (see under 'Operating Controls').

Weatherproof RCD socket

Flexible Cables

These are used to connect portable or transportable apparatus to a socket outlet by means of a plug. In many cases, eg with an electric drill or an electric dehorner, the flexible cable is connected to the appliance at the factory and should not be disconnected. Cables used to connect to single phase sockets have three cores (insulated wires), each being of different colour, or two cores where the appliance is 'double insulated', ie there is no earthing requirement. These colours, which have been standardised in Europe, and replace the former red, black and green are:

Route leads to prevent damage

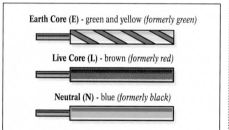

Earth Core (E) - green and yellow *(formerly green)*

Live Core (L) - brown *(formerly red)*

Neutral (N) - blue *(formerly black)*

If appliances have cables differing in colour from those described here, do not connect them before obtaining professional advice.

Cables are sized according to their current carrying capacity and must be appropriate to the appliance loading. If too small they will overheat. Braided coverings are not suitable for farm conditions; cables should be insulated with tough rubber or plastic with an overall sheath also made of the same material.

Internal connections to equipment should always be left to an approved contractor.

Extension leads using flexible cable may appear to be the most convenient method of getting a temporary supply to an area where an electrical socket has not been provided. This practice is not recommended. But if it has to be done, it is advisable that a single ready made extension lead of the correct current carrying capacity is used. In addition, care should be taken to ensure that:

▲ the extension lead is as short as possible and, if on a cable drum, is fully unreeled to prevent overheating the cable.

▲ temporary joints are not used to extend a lead. Proper connectors to BS 4343 only should be used. (Deaths have occurred because of dangerous connections to leads).

▲ the extension lead is clearly visible.

▲ routes under or around tractors or other obstacles are avoided.

▲ when the job is completed, the supply to the lead is disconnected and the lead removed.

Never put a plug on both ends of a lead.

Plugs and plug-in type connectors (single phase)

The round and flat pin plugs which fit into the appropriate sockets, each have three terminals marked E (earth), N (neutral) and L (live) to which the wires in a flexible cable are connected. The 13 amp flat pin plug may be fitted with a 2, 3, 5 or 13 amp fuse according to the load. However, for loads up to 700W the 3 amp fuse (coloured red) is usually used and for loads up to 3000W (3kW) the 13 amp fuse (coloured brown). No fuse is fitted in the old 15 amp round pin plug, or in plugs to BS 4343.

A connector socket may be fixed at the other end of a flexible cable from the plug and, provided the earth terminal is clearly marked inside the connector, a competent person able to wire a plug correctly, could also wire

up the connector. As in a plug it is vital that the cable cores be wired to the correct terminals. When selecting a plug for farm conditions it should preferably be made from high impact plastic or moulded rubber.

A plug may be rewired by a competent person and the equipment then used safely, by following the instructions in the section on 'Basic electrical tasks'.

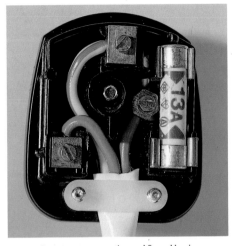

Correct, secure connections and firm cable grip

Note- see HSE Guidance Note GS37: Flexible leads, plugs and sockets etc.

Tough industrial plugs and connectors suitable for agricultural use

LIGHTING FITTINGS (LUMINAIRES)

Fluorescent lighting under cover

Electric lighting is used both for working areas and so that hazards can be seen. There are several types of lamp available; eg fluorescent, compact fluorescent and GLS tungsten filament. The lamp together with its reflector, shade and housing or enclosure is called a 'luminaire'.

A Farm Electric Handbook - *Essentials of Farm Lighting* - gives details of the different types of luminaires for use on farms. It includes recommendations on the levels of light (illuminance) for various farm situations. A Technical Information Sheet (AGR 5-2) gives installation recommendations for suitable types of luminaire in standard farm buildings.

Luminaires should be chosen to match their working situations whether indoors or outside, wet, dusty or subject to knocks. Fittings are available which will be

Floodlights for outdoor working

safe under farming conditions. Electric lighting should be installed only by a competent contractor, and this also applies to rectifying any faults.

Pendant Luminaires

A pendant luminaire consists of a ceiling rose, a short length of heat resistant flexible cable and a lampholder, together with a shade or diffuser. Both the ceiling rose and lampholder should have a means of gripping or supporting the cable sheath to prevent strain on the terminal connections. The devices may vary in different products but it is essential that they are used correctly. Nonsheathed twisted twin and nonsheathed parallel twin wires should not be used.

Installation of pendant luminaires requires great care because the ceiling rose may be live even when the light is switched off. The cable should be replaced if the insulation becomes brittle. A recommended procedure for this is given in the section on 'Basic electrical tasks'. (See page 39).

NB For all lampholders or luminaires, an earthing connection is required, necessitating a three-core heat resistant flexible cable. The earth wire must then be connected between the earthing terminals in the ceiling rose and the lampholder. In older ceiling roses earthing terminals may not have been provided in which case a metal luminaire cannot be installed.

Waterproof fittings for milking parlours

Starting fluorescents in low temperatures

Fluorescent lighting used in cold situations eg uninsulated barns, should be fitted with electronic starters. It helps to fit these starters to all fluorescent lamps because they last longer than glow starters and also extend the life of the tube.

Potato Chitting Lights

Fluorescent tubes used for chitting should be fitted with safety sheaths. These protect the user from contact with live parts should the tube be broken during use.

Safety sheath required on chitting lights

Infrared Lamps

Infrared heating lamps for livestock require special screw-type lampholders and should be fitted with protective reflectors. These luminaires need an earth conductor and should only be operated from properly earthed socket outlets.

Infrared lamps need their own sockets

They should never be connected by means of a bayonet cap adaptor to a lampholder or suspended from a ceiling rose outlet.

Flexible cables must be of the right type, ie heat-resistant and be correctly connected. Any rewiring therefore should be entrusted to a competent electrical contractor who will ensure that the lamps are correctly wired.

Cleaning

Periodic cleaning of lamps and luminaires will lengthen lamp life and improve lighting efficiency. They should be switched off and disconnected before work is started.

Discharge lamps offer low running costs

ELECTRIC HEATING

Radiant heating for broiler chicks

PIG AND POULTRY REARING

Various types of radiant heater are available for rearing young pigs and for small scale poultry farming.

The infrared lamp is intended primarily for use in pig and poultry heating. Sometimes known as a 'bright emitter' it comprises an evacuated glass envelope forming the enclosure inside which the tungsten heating element is mounted. If water drips directly on to the glass (unless it is hard glass) it can shatter and expose the live element. Infrared lamps should be of hard glass and have a protective shade over the glass envelope. Ceramic 'dull emitters' are similar but more robust than lamps. Used in the same way they give out heat but not light.

Infrared lamp and dull emitter

Where straw is used for bedding, the lamp should be mounted at least 600mm (2ft) above the straw to avoid fire risk. It is essential that the heater is attached firmly so that it cannot fall onto the stock and/or bedding.

Infrared lamps should be operated from a socket outlet system and not from a lighting circuit.

An alternative method of providing heat for young pigs or poultry is to use metal sheathed mineral

Electric heating for farm animals is discussed in detail in the Farm Electric Handbook *'Controlled Environments for Livestock'*. This chapter warns against the possible hazards associated with electric heaters used in farming and horticulture. They are reviewed under their main applications:

PIG AND POULTRY REARING

MILKING PARLOURS AND DAIRIES

CROP CONDITIONING, INCLUDING GRAIN DRYING

HORTICULTURE

FARM WORKSHOPS

VEGETABLE PACKING AND GRADING AREAS

insulated heating elements either in an overhead heater or as underfloor heating (certain flexible cables are also used for underfloor heating). Other types of overhead radiant panels and on-floor heating are available for use with livestock.

All permanent heating systems and the wiring which supplies removable heaters should be installed by a competent contractor. It is also advisable, when considering unconventional heating appliances, to consult a competent authority about their safe use, eg your Electricity Company or other approved electrical contractor.

After rearing a batch of pigs or poultry, it is normal practice to clean out before the next batch arrives. It is essential to remove all overhead or on-floor heaters (which should be supplied from hoseproof sockets) before any steam or pressure washing is carried out and to clean them separately.

MILKING PARLOURS AND DAIRIES

Quartz linear lamp (QLL) heaters and metal sheathed infrared heaters are often installed to provide comfort heating for stockmen working in the parlour pit. Care should be taken to avoid splashing these heaters when cleaning down after milking. All heaters should be switched off before cleaning takes place. Radiant heaters with exposed wire elements of the domestic type must never be used in the damp conditions of a milking parlour.

QLLs are well suited to milking parlours

To provide frost protection for water pipes in dairies and parlours, quartz linear lamp heaters and heating cables can be used. To operate heating

Heated creeps in farrowing room

cables efficiently, thermal insulation should be placed over the cables and pipework, and the cables controlled by a thermostat. For safety the cable should be mechanically protected where livestock have access to it. An RCD should be installed as an electrical safety measure. In addition the cables could be operated at low voltage (eg 7V) from a suitably enclosed isolating transformer.

QLLs also used at lambing

CROP CONDITIONING INCLUDING GRAIN DRYING

Electric heater banks and dehumidifiers are used with electric fans for grain drying. Manufacturers normally provide an interlocking arrangement which prevents the heaters from coming on without the fan. In addition an overriding thermostat on the fan casing disconnects the heater bank if the fan motor burns out or stops. When considering crop conditioning, check that the safety devices are included. Before the start of the grain drying season the drier should be inspected thoroughly for any damage and tested for safety. To avoid the risk of fire or element burn out, it should be cleaned and the heater banks blown clear of accumulated dust.

QLL heaters in a farm workshop

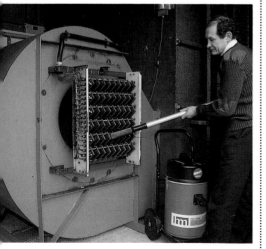

Blow or vacuum to clean heater banks before drying (shown with guard removed)

HORTICULTURE

In greenhouses where soil warming cables are used on the floor or in benches, these should be provided with a continuous earthed sheath, and connection boxes should be watertight. Various types of flexible foil or neoprene rubber sheathed heating mats may also be used for soil warming. These should be operated at low voltage (eg 24V) from a suitably enclosed isolating transformer. When cleaning or repairing benches, always check that the mains switch to the warming installation is off before starting work. RCD protection should be included where mains voltage soil warming cable is used.

FARM WORKSHOPS

Most farm workshops and machinery servicing areas are uninsulated and fairly open structures in which it is difficult to provide heating for those carrying out maintenance work. Quartz linear lamp (QLL) heaters, by providing beams of warmth which penetrate damp air, are ideal for heating farm workshops or machinery service areas. They can be directed to specific areas of work and provide instant warmth. They should be mounted at the correct height, out of the way of mobile equipment and should not come into contact with water.

Low voltage soil warming cables and transformers

QLLs directed to key working positions

British Standard 5502 (Part 80), Code of Practice for Design and Construction of Workshops, Maintenance and Inspection Facilities, states "it may be necessary to provide infrared heat in certain uninsulated buildings. Quartz linear heaters should be used for this purpose."

They are particularly effective in packhouses where the produce has been chilled, as they heat the staff without warming the chilled produce.

VEGETABLE PACKING AND GRADING AREAS

QLL heaters directed to key working positions in vegetable packhouses or on potato or fruit grading lines can provide cold weather comfort for staff while minimising deterioration of the crops.

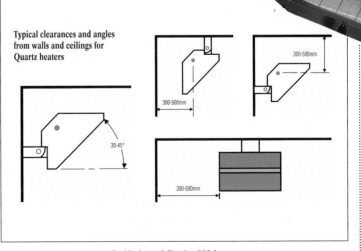

Typical clearances and angles from walls and ceilings for Quartz heaters

300-500mm

300-500mm

30-45°

300-500mm

Positioning and directing QLL heaters

ELECTRIC MOTORS AND POWER EQUIPMENT

Motor for feed preparation

The Electricity at Work Regulations require that equipment should be constructed so as to resist the entry of dust and dirt where this may give rise to electrical and mechanical failure. Regular inspection and cleaning as necessary is recommended where dirt and dusts are likely to accumulate. In general it is wise to use totally enclosed fan ventilated motors for every application in farming and horticulture.

In milling plants where fine grinding of cereals is carried out, it is important to use motors with high standards of dustproofing; although for most farm feed preparation plants the totally enclosed motor is adequate. Machinery manufacturers usually select the motors, but where for example, a purchase is made at a sale and the motor is changed or fitted afterwards, make sure it is of the totally enclosed type and of the correct rating. Thermal protection of the motors needs to be properly arranged and should be undertaken by a competent contractor. Overload 'trips' should be set by the contractor when installing a motor and if adjustments become necessary they should only be done by a person qualified to carry out this task.

Fan capacitor in waterproof housing

Remember the requirement under the Agriculture (Stationary Machinery) Regulations for adequate guarding of motors and associated belt and pulley drives. This does not apply to direct drive ventilating fan motors which are mounted in the ridge of a building and away from accidental contact by personnel, but guarding must be provided for fans mounted in walls of buildings.

Maintenance of motors is often neglected because they run with so little trouble, but a regular cleaning programme for both motors and control gear is needed. Dust which can lead to overheating and fires should not be allowed to accumulate. Cleaning can well be repaid by fewer burnouts and longer motor life. Cleaning should include using suction to remove dust, meal etc as powerful blowers are liable to build up internal accumulations instead of removing them. Routine maintenance should be carried out in accordance with the manufacturer's instructions.

Where motors are used only seasonally, eg for crop dryers, there may be a risk of shafts rusting or bearing grease collecting and hardening at the lowest points in the casings. To counteract this, such motors should be run for say, 15-30 minutes every three months. Running should be more frequent where motors are kept in damp conditions.

When single phase fan motors have separate capacitors (condensers), they should be mounted in waterproof enclosures so as to meet the requirement for protection against weather, wet, dirty, dusty or corrosive conditions.

SAFETY CONTROLS

Isolating switches

Under the Agriculture (Stationary Machinery) Regulations 'every prime mover (electric motor in this context) must have a readily accessible device (eg a switch), by which it can quickly be stopped. This device must be on or near the prime mover, unless the prime mover is more than 2 metres (6ft 6in) from places to which a worker has access, or is otherwise situated so as to prevent the worker from coming into contact with it'. Each switch must be clearly marked to show which motor it controls.

Under these regulations, a switch may include a starter. But to comply with the IEE Regulations, if it is necessary to have a starter remote from the motor, an additional isolating switch must also be installed close to the motor. This is particularly important with grain elevators and conveyors as well as for ventilating fans automatically controlled through remote panels or thermostats.

equipment and for the isolation of the electrical equipment.

The second regulation requires that there must be suitable means of ensuring that the supply will remain switched off and inadvertent reconnection prevented.

Main air ducts of some drying plants can be dangerous if such care is overlooked. Interlocks should be provided so that when the duct lighting is switched on, the fan motor is inoperative.

In the case of fan ventilation of livestock buildings, special care is necessary where a group of fan motors is under temperature control from a single control panel. Where control panels for fans do not incorporate mains isolators, these must be provided by the contractor.

The Electricity at Work Regulations require that, where necessary to prevent danger, suitable means, including methods of identifying circuits, shall be available for cutting off the supply of electricity to the

The installer must pay attention to and carry out the fan manufacturer's instructions regarding provision of alarms and fail-safe devices. The farmer should satisfy himself that adequate alarms, fail-safe devices and/or stand-by generators are installed. Once this equipment is in, all concerned should understand the action necessary to deal with an emergency and the alarm should be tested regularly, say once a month.

Fan control

Resistance regulators should never be used for controlling fan speeds nor indeed for lighting control. They constitute a fire hazard.

Typical stop devices

PORTABLE AND TRANSPORTABLE EQUIPMENT

A variety of portable electrical equipment is used on farms including electric drills and dehorners. Portable equipment is potentially more dangerous than fixed appliances: its portability makes it liable to be thrown about, dropped and stored just where it was last used. Portable electric equipment is perfectly safe provided it is carefully selected for the job it has to do, properly maintained

Good storage prevents damage

and used sensibly. Wherever possible portable equipment should be double insulated and approved by BEAB, BSI or an equivalent approval body. Where practicable the handles of portable equipment should be of insulating material.

It is essential to have portable equipment serviced on a regular basis by a person competent to do so. See *HSE Guidance Note PM32: Safe use of portable electrical apparatus.*

Where there are adverse conditions eg in the wet or where mechanical damage is likely, it is advisable to use reduced voltage apparatus, eg 110V or less. Remember that animals are even more sensitive to electric shock than humans. Low voltage equipment requires transformers which reduce the mains voltage to a safe value, lessening the danger of serious electric shock . 110V supplies from such transformers are isolated from the mains supply and have an earthed centre tap so that the maximum voltage to earth is only 55V.

See *HSE Guidance Note PM29: Electrical hazards from steam/water pressure cleaners etc.*

If it is not possible to operate the equipment at reduced voltage, the socket outlets should be protected by means of 30mA RCDs. The flexible cable is the most vulnerable part of 240V rated equipment. A damaged or worn flexible lead is dangerous. Regular inspection of double insulated equipment is just as important as it is for earthed equipment. Before using any portable equipment it should be visually examined, especially the flexible cable and plug, to see that it is in sound condition and free from obvious damage.

Check plugs and cables before use

GENERATORS

Generators are frequently used for emergency, stand-by or convenience purposes. Generator sets vary in size from a few hundred watts for domestic purposes, to much higher rated sets for commerce and industry.

Unless correctly installed and operated, all generators, large or small, are potentially dangerous, not only on the sites where they are used but also at locations to which they may become connected. There are statutory requirements associated with the connection of generators to electrical installations. It is essential that the installation of private generators is carried out by competent electrical contractors who will ensure that all the necessary safety measures are observed.

Your local Electricity Company would be pleased to help.

See *HSE Guidance Note PM53: Emergency private generation: electrical safety*.

Stand-by generator for dairy

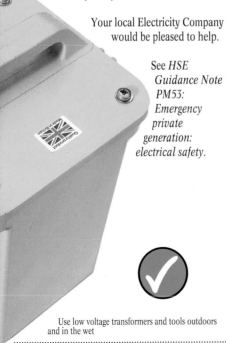

Use low voltage transformers and tools outdoors and in the wet

ELECTRIC FENCES

Electric fence controllers should conform to BS 2632, 6167 or 6369. Mains operated fence units should only be installed by a competent electrical contractor. Every earth electrode connected to the earth terminal of an electric fence must be separate and should not be connected to any other earthing system. No more than one controller should be connected to each electric fence. Read the instructions supplied with the controller before erecting the fence.

The erection of electric fences near or under overhead power lines should be avoided. When a fence has to be erected near a power line, avoid a route parallel to the line since this could result in dangerous voltages being induced in the fence. A route at right-angles to the line minimises this danger. Under no circumstances should barbed wire be connected to an electricity source. Electric fences are more effective when kept clear of vegetation.

Great care must also be exercised when putting up fence wires under overhead lines especially on hillsides. Any whipping or upward movement of the wire may take it dangerously close to the power line.

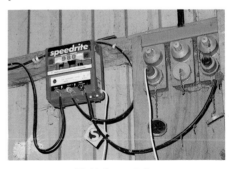

Electric fence controller

Anchor fence securely at several points

The fence should be securely anchored at several points to avoid the possibility, when the wire is tensioned, of a single anchor pulling out and the suddenly released wire contacting an overhead power line. Electric fences erected near public rights of way should be fitted with suitable warning notices at frequent intervals so that each is visible from its neighbour.

Electric fences to be well signed

ELECTRIC ARC WELDING

Electric arc welding may be powered either by alternating or direct current. An alternating current (a.c.) supply is obtained from a transformer; a direct current (d.c.) supply may be obtained either from a transformer and rectifier, a converter, or a generator. Output voltages from welding sets may be as high as 100V on a.c. sets and 80V on d.c. sets. In general, welding by direct current is safer than by alternating current and is preferred in damp or harsh environments.

During welding care must be taken to avoid electric shock or burns by contact with parts of the electrode holder or the live electrode. All-insulated electrode holders are recommended.

The principal components of the welding circuit are:

▲ the welding lead which carries current from the welding set to the electrode and the work.

▲ the welding return which carries the current returning from the work to the welding set.

Currents of 300 amp or more are required for welding; all parts of the circuit must therefore be of adequate conductivity. A welding return lead is essential; never rely on fortuitous return paths via structural steelwork, metal pipes, etc, which can result in electric shock or fire.

The electric arc produces heat rays which can cause painful 'sunburn' on exposed skin and ultra-violet light which is harmful to unprotected eyes. The welder's eyes must be protected by a suitable filter lens contained in a welding helmet or hand-held face shield which protects the face and neck against heat. Eye damage from not using a welding shield is permanent. The hands and forearms should be protected by wearing suitable gloves and by keeping sleeves rolled down. Gas welding goggles are unsuitable for protecting the eyes against the intense light emitted by an electric arc.

The welding operation must be suitably screened to protect the eyes of people in the vicinity who might be at risk from exposure to the arc.

Always use gloves and shield

For more detailed guidance refer to *HSE Guidance Note PM64: Electrical safety in arc welding (revised 1991).*

OVERHEAD LINE HAZARDS

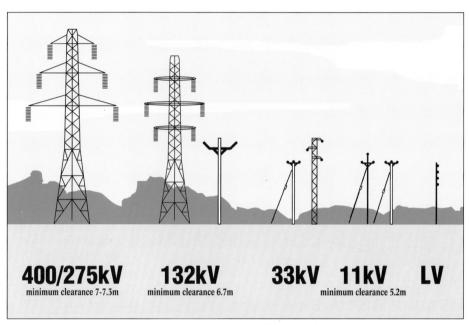

400/275kV
minimum clearance 7-7.3m

132kV
minimum clearance 6.7m

33kV 11kV LV
minimum clearance 5.2m

Transmission towers (pylons), poles and cable-to-ground clearances

Contact with overhead power lines causes serious injuries every year; a third of such inadvertent contacts have proved to be fatal. The majority of accidents have occurred through the failure to notice the lines and to take sensible preventative measures. Larger farm machinery has increased the risk of such accidents.

This section sets out the main precautions that should be taken when working in the vicinity of overhead lines. They are dealt with in detail in *HSE Guidance Note GS6: Avoidance of danger from overhead electric lines.*

DANGERS ASSOCIATED WITH OVERHEAD LINES

Making contact or near contact with overhead electric lines is highly dangerous; one in three accidents is fatal. Lines carrying voltages as high as 400,000 volts or as low as 240 volts must be treated with equal respect. As the voltage increases it is necessary to keep further away from the line.

Electric power lines supported on wood poles are often mistaken for telegraph lines. This is a dangerous assumption. Wood poles carrying lines operating at 132,000 volts are not uncommon. Statutory requirements specify minimum clearances for overhead lines and for lines at up to 33,000 volts the minimum height required is 5.2m (17ft).

Overhead electric wires are normally bare (uninsulated) and if contact is made by an irrigator boom, a water jet, bale loader, forklift truck, metal pipe or ladder, fishing rod, hand tool or any other similar object, then an electric current will discharge with a high risk of fatal or severe shock and burns to any person nearby.

It is dangerous even to be close to overhead lines eg when pruning trees. At all times treat overhead lines as a hazard and assume they are uninsulated.

50 metre towers keep HV lines out of danger

Variables such as the type of overhead line, its route, the type of agricultural equipment or vehicle, the nature of the terrain, all make it impracticable to specify a minimum working clearance from overhead lines which would be safe in all circumstances.

The danger from overhead lines can be reduced if sensible precautions and safe working procedures are followed in consultation with the operators of overhead lines, who are generally the Electricity Companies. The advice given below is to help meet these requirements.

GENERAL PRECAUTIONS

Ensure that all persons on the farm who may be affected by the presence of overhead lines are aware of the dangers. Know the routes of overhead lines. All high voltage poles should carry warning signs.

▲ Never reduce the clearance under overhead lines by dumping or tipping of waste material, landscaping, erecting structures, building haystacks or creating storage areas.

▲ Avoid operating plant in any situation where contact or near contact with an overhead line is possible.

▲ Erect barriers to prevent vehicles and plant

This is not a telegraph pole

Transformer on single wooden pole

Never reduce clearances under overhead lines

contacting lines and damaging poles and their stays.

▲ Only move ladders, elevators, pipes or other long objects horizontally and in the lowest position.

▲ Keep overhead lines in view when manoeuvring mobile plant.

▲ Special care and planning should be exercised when moving large items of plant from one part of the farm to another, especially tall machines or machines having long booms. See section on 'Irrigation and slurry equipment' for more detail.

▲ Never light fires or allow them to burn under or near overhead lines.

▲ Take care with tractor mounted hedge trimmers under power lines or close to pole stays. Damaged stays must be reported to the Electricity Company.

DON'T USE CARBON FIBRE RODS OR POLES NEAR OVERHEAD ELECTRIC POWER LINES

IT COULD BE FATAL

Look Out! Look Up! Be aware of overhead lines

▲ Never assume that overhead conductors which have fallen or are caught in a tree are dead. NO attempt should be made to remove fallen trees from overhead lines; the wires could still be live. Report all incidents to the local Electricity Company as soon as possible.

▲ Do not allow anyone to fish, sail or camp anywhere near overhead lines

▲ At all times 'Look Out, Look Up and keep clear of overhead power lines'

VEHICLE ACCIDENTS

Should a vehicle or its attachments come into contact with a power line, the greatest danger arises if someone were to make contact between the vehicle and earth. Usually the driver will remain safe within his cab.

▲ Do not touch the vehicle or anything attached to it.

Know the routes of all overhead lines

Never assume fallen lines are dead

▲ Get the Electricity Company to disconnect the power as quickly as possible.

▲ If the vehicle is not tangled in the wire and is still operating, it can carefully be backed away and the contact broken. Similarly a tipper can carefully be lowered or a high lift attachment can carefully be withdrawn.

▲ If the driver needs to leave the vehicle he must literally jump clear and must not link the vehicle to the ground. He must not go back to the vehicle. Even if it appears safe to do so, automatic switching of the power lines can reconnect the line and the vehicle will be dangerously live.

▲ No one should touch the vehicle until it is certain that the power has been disconnected.

▲ Do not rely on the vehicle's rubber tyres or rubber soled boots to provide any protection from electric shock.

LOOK OUT, LOOK UP - keep clear of overhead lines

Do not touch the vehicle or anything attached to it

IRRIGATION AND SLURRY SPRAYING

Where irrigation is carried out near power lines, there may be a risk to persons and to the security of the electricity supply unless proper precautions are taken. Accidents, some fatal, have occurred due to insufficient working clearance from the lines during automatic operation, mechanical failures of the machines, contact with the lines during transportation and careless handling of associated pipework. In addition, conductor clashing, resulting in loss of supply, has been caused by the impact of water jets on overhead power lines.

Irrigation machinery is dealt with in more detail on page 33.

SAFETY PRECAUTIONS FOR IRRIGATION EQUIPMENT

▲ Remember high voltage conductors are normally bare and are not insulated against contact from pressurised water spray. Therefore water pressure should be kept as low as possible.

▲ Plan the route to be taken when moving tall and long machines. Consult your Electricity Company and discuss the proposed routes to ensure that no hazards will arise from the presence of overhead lines. Attention is drawn to *HSE Guidance Note GS6: Avoidance of danger from overhead electric lines.*

▲ Never carry out any work (such as repairs or adjustments) while a machine is under, or is in close proximity to, an overhead power line. If a machine breaks down, the water should be turned off and the machine towed at least 15m (50ft) away from the line (where applicable with booms under close control).

▲ Take care when installing a piped water supply. Pipes should always be carried in a horizontal position and as near to the ground as practicable. DO NOT leave them where children or others could lift them into an electric line. Pipes should be chained up if possible.

▲ Where irrigation machines could be dangerous, consider the use of sprinkler systems. The nozzles of these systems must be kept at least 3 metres from directly underneath high voltage conductors, including those on wood poles.

▲ In the event of a mishap, if any part of a machine or pipe touches or is close to an overhead power line, KEEP AWAY from it until the Electricity Company has confirmed that it is safe to approach.

▲ If suitable warning notices are not already fitted, then machines should display the Electricity Association black and yellow warning label 'Beware - Overhead Electric Power Lines' (obtainable through your Electricity Company).

All operators should have a copy of the pocket card *'Irrigators and Overhead Power Lines - Operators' Safety Guide'*, from your local Electricity Company.

The addresses and telephone numbers of the local offices of the Electricity Company may be found in the telephone directory under 'Electricity'.

Note: Publicity material in the form of leaflets, pocket cards, warning stickers are available from

Electricity Companies or the Electricity Association Safety Group at :
30 Millbank, London SW1P 4RD
Telephone: 071-834 2333

Avoid unloading near power lines and always carry pipes in the horizontal position

CB RADIO AERIALS

Unfortunately there have been a number of fatal accidents involving the contact of radio aerials with overhead lines. It is essential to take great care when erecting aerials and when using them on tractors or combine harvesters.

Avoid areas where there are overhead lines. It is difficult to estimate the height of an overhead line and therefore a safety margin should always be provided to let the aerial pass underneath.

Check for overhead lines before fishing

Short radio aerials eliminate danger of contact

Also guard against the accidental falling of an aerial on to electrical lines or equipment. The height of aerials on vehicles with radio telephones must also take into account the possibility of contact with overhead lines.

FISHING

Several people have died and others have been seriously injured through using carbon fibre fishing rods and poles near overhead electric power lines.

The following advice is designed to prevent these accidents.

▲ Because rods and poles containing carbon fibre conduct electricity well, they are particularly dangerous when used near overhead electric power lines. Remember that electricity can jump gaps and a rod does not even have to touch an electric line to cause a lethal current to flow.

▲ Many overhead electric power lines are supported by wood poles which could be mistaken for telegraph poles. These lines may carry electricity at up to 132,000 volts.

▲ The legal height of overhead electric power lines can be as low as 5.2m (17ft) and they are therefore within easy reach of a carbon fibre rod or pole. Remember that overhead lines may not be readily visible from the ground. They may be concealed by hedges or by a dark background. Make sure you 'Look Out' and 'Look Up' to check for overhead lines before fishing begins. In general, the minimum safe fishing distance from an overhead electric power line is two rod or pole lengths from the overhead line (measured along the ground).

Hold fishing matches well away from power lines

▲ When pegging out for matches or competitions, organisers and competitors should, in general, ensure that no peg is nearer to an overhead electric power line than 30 metres (measured along the ground).

▲ For further advice on safe fishing at specific locations please contact your local Electricity Company.

Store dinghies well away from power lines

SAILING

Sailing boats and dinghies are frequently fitted with aluminium masts and on most craft metal wires are used as stays. Both of these are good conductors and can therefore cause danger if they come close to overhead power lines. Care should be taken to prevent sailing under low power lines and additionally when transporting or manoeuvring boats near electric wires. Do not store boats on farms near lines.

Look Out, Look Up - keep clear of overhead lines

▲ Finally, remember that it is dangerous for any object to get too close to overhead power lines, particularly if the object is an electrical conductor eg a lead cored fishing line, or damp fishing line or rod.

CAMPING & KITES

Do not allow camping near overhead lines because tent poles, stays or guy ropes could come into contact with live conductors and cause dangerous currents to flow through anyone touching them. Do not use stays as washing lines. Kites should never be flown near power lines for the same reason. If a kite escapes and becomes tangled in power lines do not attempt to retrieve it and do not touch the kite string but notify the Electricity Company.

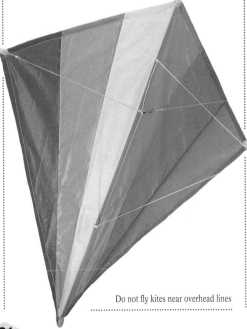

Do not fly kites near overhead lines

UNDERGROUND CABLE HAZARDS

Many accidents are caused by hand and machine tools, fence posts or spikes hitting underground cables. This type of accident can cause electric shock and arcing may occur resulting in serious burns.

Electric cables are laid at varying depths, according to voltage rating and situation, with a minimum depth of 450mm. However, it must not be assumed that cables will not be found within 450mm of the surface since variations in ground level often occur after the cables have been laid.

Cable down the pole indicates presence of underground cables

Some cables are covered by a layer of concrete or tiles placed about 50mm above them. Although these provide some mechanical protection, their main purpose is to give warning of the presence of cables. Plastic marker tape may also be used for this purpose.

It is clearly necessary to know the location of cables on the farm, your Electricity Company will be able to help in this

Know the location of underground cables

respect. Put up warning notices at all suitable spots where the presence of underground cables is known. The cables may have an outer covering of PVC and can easily be mistaken for water pipes. Before excavations are started a check should be made to ensure that no underground cables are present.

Check to see if cables are running down overhead line poles as this is an indication that underground cables are present. Special instruments are available for locating the position of underground cables. If they are exposed, do not attempt to move them without first consulting the local Electricity Company.

If a cable is accidentally damaged, then however slight the damage may be, the incident should be reported to the Electricity Company. Minor damage to a cable can develop into a serious fault at a later stage and result in loss of supply.

See *HS(G) 47: Avoiding danger from underground services,* from the Health and Safety Executive.

No spikes or posts near underground cables

IRRIGATION AND SLURRY EQUIPMENT

Machinery for irrigating and spreading slurry presents its own particular problems when used near overhead power lines. Jets of water can conduct electric currents and liquid slurry is an even better conductor. Thus spraying devices could become live if the jets were to come into contact with overhead lines. Also these liquids must be prevented from entering or coating electrical equipment where they could cause short circuits and corrosion.

This section deals with the commonly used irrigation machines and the precautions that should be taken with them.

Low Precipitation Sprinklers

These use rotating sprinklers attached at various points along a static main.

Care should be taken when laying out pipe systems

for sprinklers. Pipes normally made of light aluminium and up to 9m (30ft) long, should always be carried in a horizontal position and as near the ground as practicable. DO NOT leave them where the public or children might gain access. These precautions should also be followed when installing water supply piping for other types of irrigators.

Avoid spraying electric lines and equipment

Rain Gun

This normally consists of a high pressure water nozzle mounted on a carriage and connected to a large drum by a flexible hose up to 400 metres (1,300ft) long.

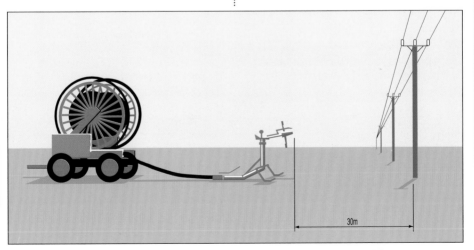

30m

Typical arrangement of rain gun (not to scale): rain guns should travel parallel to overhead lines

As the drum rotates, the hose retracts drawing the rain gun backwards in a straight line. Typically the jet of water achieves a throw of about 70 metres (230ft) reaching a height of about 15 metres (50ft). The nozzle can rotate in a horizontal plane through a pre-set angle (normally about 270º).

Rain guns can incorporate jet break-up devices although these can become or be made inoperative. Any jet must be broken up before reaching an overhead power line, and for this purpose ring nozzles are more effective than taper nozzles. Where an 'interrupter' is fitted it should work correctly but will not of itself provide sufficient jet break-up.

Low volume irrigator

Wherever practicable, a rain gun should travel parallel to an overhead power line rather than pass under it. If it is essential for a machine to pass under a power line, specific safety arrangements must be agreed with the Electricity Company.

If the overall height of the machine (or drum) is over 4 metres (13ft) special consideration should be given to approved routes using marker posts, 'goal posts' etc.

Slurry Guns

These are usually rain guns adapted for spraying liquid manure. Liquid manure may also be spread by tankers or applied by long boom irrigators described below.

Slurry guns are often fitted with large nozzles (25mm diameter minimum) and sometimes made of rubber. The liquid manure is pumped to the slurry gun through normal irrigation pipes.

The conductivity of liquid manure is higher than that of water. If a jet from a slurry gun makes contact with electrical equipment, the risk is that unsafe leakage currents will pass down the jet to earth and through the body of anyone in contact with the machine. A high density spray depositing solids onto conductors and insulators can lead to a breakdown of insulation and flashover which could damage equipment and interrupt electricity supplies. In addition, solid residues on lines can give rise to severe radio and TV interference.

Liquid manure, particularly from livestock, can be corrosive and could have long-term effects on the mechanical and electrical performance of power supply equipment.

All forms of liquid manure, particularly where sprayed from slurry guns or tankers, should be kept well clear of electrical plant and overhead lines of any voltage.

The prime safety precaution is that the slurry gun must not be used nearer to an overhead line than a horizontal clearance equal to the maximum throw of the jet. This distance must be increased in high winds to take account of increased projection by 'windblow' effects.

Long Boom Irrigators

The boom is constructed of a large lattice metal framework mounted at its mid-point on wheels. The arms of the frame are essentially water pipes with multiple fixed sprinklers along their length, sometimes with a larger jet at one or both ends.

Secure boom before manoeuvring

Some machines have fixed booms and travel slowly during automatic operation, others with rotating booms, remain stationary. The framework has an overall span of up to 80 metres (262ft) and a height, when set up for operation, of up to 5.6 metres (18ft 6in). The minimum height of some machines is about 5 metres (17ft) and this is exceeded by others which have booms that are folded and then raised vertically.

Generally, the advice given by Electricity Companies will be that a minimum horizontal clearance of 15 metres (50ft) from the tip of the boom to the nearest overhead electric power line should be maintained.

It is dangerous to move any long boom under an overhead power line. Uneven or sloping ground can cause large movements of the boom tips, particularly when passing through gateways etc.

> **WHEN MOVING IN THE VICINITY OF OVERHEAD POWER LINES APPROVED ACCESS ROUTES MUST BE USED**

Routes should be agreed with the Electricity Company and marked on site if necessary. The machine should be kept under direct observation and control. If the booms have not been dismantled before moving they must be set fore and aft, with a nylon control rope used by a person positioned at each end. If assembly or dismantling is to be carried out on site, it should be done well outside the 15 metres (50ft) safety clearance

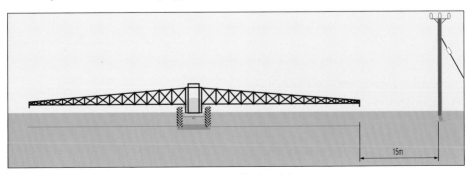

Typical arrangement of long boom irrigator

described previously. If the irrigator is mobile, the selected path of travel should not pass under an overhead power line. If necessary, the path should be marked on site so that safety clearances can be maintained.

The sprinkler jet normally used is unlikely to interfere with the overhead power lines but many machines have a single large jet from one end which could reach the line. In such cases, the jet should be checked to ensure that it is broken into droplets before contact is made. The machine should be mechanically sound and correctly maintained, failure could result in an accident.

Always carry pipes in horizontal position, as low as possible

Check location of all overhead electric power lines before moving or using machines

GENERAL PRECAUTIONS

The operator of these machines has responsibility for the safety both of his own employees and others who may be affected by the work. Electricity Companies can offer constructive advice to enable the machines to be used with safety in the vicinity of overhead electric lines. Field tests have established that the most important precaution to be taken with irrigators and slurry guns of all types is to:

> ENSURE THAT NO PART OF THE EQUIPMENT COMES WITHIN 30 METRES (100ft), MEASURED HORIZONTALLY AT GROUND LEVEL, OF AN OVERHEAD ELECTRIC POWER LINE.

If it is necessary for any part of the equipment to be brought within 30 metres you should CONSULT YOUR LOCAL ELECTRICITY COMPANY FIRST.

Consultation on site with the Electricity Company, together with the adoption of sensible precautions, may permit irrigation equipment to approach or operate closer to overhead power lines than the consultation distance specified above.

BASIC ELECTRICAL TASKS

Farmers and growers are practical people and therefore it should be within their competence, safely to undertake some basic repairs to single phase equipment. But if there are any doubts, help should be sought from a competent electrician.

Assemble a basic tool kit, always use the proper tools

Always use proper tools including correctly sized screwdrivers and purpose-made wire strippers.

Preparing a flexible cable

Prepare a flexible cable for connection to a single phase plug, connector or lamp fitting by following this procedure:

1 Mark off the length of inner cable cores to be exposed, cut and strip off outer sheath - taking care not to nick the insulation of the inner cable cores.

2 Cut off any threads between cores.

3 Measure and mark off the exact length of each core for connection to relevant terminals. (Earth is usually the longest)

4 Strip off only sufficient insulation from each core to allow the cores to enter and be fixed to the terminals. Take care not to nick the wires, use a proper wire stripper. Twist the wire strands of each core tightly before inserting into terminals and leave no stray strands exposed.

5 Check wires are held firmly in the terminals.

Never fit a plug to both ends of a flexible cable.

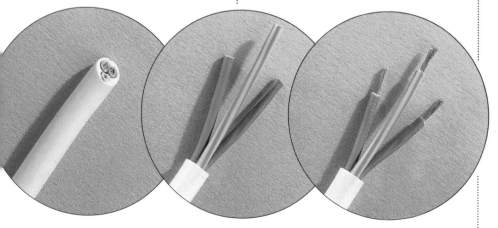

Preparing the end of a flexible cable

Wiring a plug or connector

A plug may be rewired and the equipment then used safely by following this procedure:

1 Check that the plug is disconnected from the supply.

2 Remove the cover, taking care to retain the screw(s).

3 If there is a cable clamp, remove one of the fixing screws and loosen the other.
Note: some plugs have press-in grips for the cable.

4 Remove or slacken all terminal screws as appropriate. (In some types, the fuse has to be removed to gain access to the live terminal).

5 Prepare the flexible cable as described above.

6 Position cable to reach all terminals and to ensure the clamp can be secured over the outer sheath.

7 Connect prepared core ends to terminals as follows:

Green/yellow to E (earth) usually sited top centre.
Blue to N (neutral) usually sited on left.
Brown to L (live) usually sited on right.

Note: with some forms of connection, core end loops are used. (The loops can be preformed around a small screwdriver and positioned clockwise on the terminals, to minimise unravelling of strands when the screws are tightened).

8 Tighten screws securely and ensure that no bare wire shows outside terminals.

9 Tighten the cable clamp so as to grip the outer sheath of the cable or make sure sheath is held in press-in grips.

10 Where applicable, insert correct size cartridge fuse.

11 Replace cover and retaining screw(s).

Warning:
If the colours in the flexible cable differ from those described here, the plug terminals are unmarked, or it is a three phase installation, do not attempt the wiring, but seek professional advice. This is especially important for three phase equipment.

Wiring a plug or connector

Replacing a pendant flexible cable

There are several types of ceiling rose and lampholder, but all consist of two basic parts: a body containing terminals and a cover for the terminals. A pendant lampholder has two or three terminals, a ceiling rose may have three or four.

It is important therefore, to note carefully which terminals are used for the cable connections.

If the insulation of a flexible cable becomes brittle, or the lampholder shows signs of deterioration, it should be replaced. Any large scale renovation of this kind should be carried out by a competent electrician, but an urgent replacement of a single flexible cable may be carried out safely by following this procedure:

1 Switch on at the local switch to check that the lamp works and leave it on.

2 Switch off supply to fuse-board and check that the light has gone off. Remove fuse (and keep it in your possession) or switch off circuit breaker controlling the relevant lighting circuit.

> **Caution:** Ceiling rose may be LIVE even when light is switched off

3 Place a notice at the switch indicating that maintenance is in progress.

4 Remove lamp and shade.

5 Unscrew ceiling rose cover. Make a note which terminals are used, and loosen screws to disconnect the flexible cable.

6 Unscrew lampholder cover; loosen terminal screws and remove cable.

7 Prepare both ends of new flexible cable as described above.

8 Pass one end of cable through the lampholder cover and connect cores to the holder terminals. Replace cover.

9 Pass other end of the cable through ceiling rose cover and connect the cores to appropriate terminals in the ceiling rose.

Note: always use the cable support devices provided in ceiling roses and lampholders.

10 Replace cover.

11 Replace shade or diffuser, using retainer provided.

12 Replace lamp .

13 Replace circuit fuse, then switch on again to restore current to all circuits.

Wiring a pendant flexible cable

OPERATING CONTROLS

Electrical equipment can easily be controlled and this can reduce running costs. This section sets out advice on the types of controls for motors, heating and lighting, their installation, use and maintenance. Ventilation and heating control systems for livestock houses are described here but their detailed design is covered in the Farm Electric Handbook *'Controlled Environments for Livestock'*.

Hoseproof switch for loads up to 20 amps

MOTOR CONTROLS

Small motors of less than 0.37kW (0.5hp) may be switched direct on line (DOL) from a fixed socket outlet, but motors larger than 0.37kW should be switched by a starter permanently wired into the supply. Starters protect the motor against overload or low voltage by switching off when these occur. Some also control starting currents electro-mechanically. Three phase motors, eg those used on compressors for milk cooling, should additionally be protected against damage from 'single phasing' due to a failure of one of the phases. This protection should be incorporated in the motor starter.

For some applications electronic 'soft start' starters are now available which reduce starting currents.

Typical motor stop/start control

HEATER CONTROLS

Heaters of up to 3kW can be switched from sockets outlets of 13, 15 or 16 amps. The sockets must be protected against animal contact. In these cases suitable cord-operated switches mounted at high level can help. Heaters of more than 3kW need special sockets capable of carrying higher currents and in some cases, switching may be by a contactor. The choice of control is a matter for advice from the electrical contractor.

Other controls include: thermostats, humidistats, electronic thermostats, energy regulators, and timing devices.

For the selection and installation of any of these you should rely on the advice of an approved contractor. Some helpful points to bear in mind are below.

Thermostats

For general temperature control the vapour pressure type using a capillary tube is suitable since the sensor bulb can be placed in the best position.

In a greenhouse where direct sunlight may fall on the sensor, an aspirated thermostat (which has a shield) is used to protect it from solar gain. It contains a small fan which draws air from the house over the sensor providing a continuous sample

Capillary thermostat

Aspirated screen (thermostat) for greenhouses

for the thermostat. Never use a so-called room-type thermostat where a really accurate control of temperature is important because (a) if mounted on a wall it rarely responds to the true average air temperature in the building, and (b) it is not sufficiently sensitive to changes in greenhouse temperature.

academic importance. Maintenance of thermostats involves regularly removing dust from the sensing element, preferably by an air jet, so that its sensitivity to temperature changes is retained.

Digital electronic thermostat

Electronic thermostats

Electronic thermostats using solid-state circuitry operate more accurately than capillary or mechanical thermostats. These circuits are often in removable modules and it is as well to have spare modules available in case they fail. Availability of spares should be checked with the manufacturer or the installing contractor.

In use, the settings of a thermostat should always be checked against an accurate thermometer (preferably the max. and min. type) placed close to the sensing element. The temperature shown by the thermometer will enable any difference between this and the thermostat setting to be allowed for.

Heat and ventilation controls for poultry house

Humidistats

Humidistats used to control humidity are somewhat specialised; it is important to follow the manufacturer's instructions for their installation and maintenance.

The livestock farmer knows that for maximum productivity of his stock (especially pigs and poultry) the temperature must be precisely controlled. A lower temperature than optimum can send the food consumption and bills soaring; up to 80% of his costs can be feed. Keeping temperatures in buildings within optimum limits is of economic not just of

Sensor for high/low temperature alarm

Energy Regulators

Energy regulators are not thermostats, ie are not sensitive to temperature. They adjust the energy input according to the control knob setting. The domestic versions give comparatively coarse control and appropriate settings for particular purposes are learned by experience. Sensitive energy regulators of industrial standard are more appropriate to many farming or growing applications, eg the manual control of heating.

Timing Devices

There are simple repeat cycle timers which automatically repeat ON/OFF cycles in specific time periods, say every 15, 30 or 60 minutes. Or time switches which rotate once daily or weekly and within the single rotation enable a number of ON/OFF cycles to occur and to be varied when required. More recently programmable electronic time switches have also become available.

Programmable timer keypad

Time switches are particularly useful in poultry houses and in dairies for example, to ensure that water is heated during cheaper electricity periods to reduce running costs. It is recommended that a time switch incorporating a spring or battery reserve is used. Remember, after an electricity supply interruption, to correct the time switch if it does not have reserve. Programmable time switches always have a reserve.

Timers switch pumps on during cheaper electricity periods

LIGHTING CONTROLS

It is particularly important where lights are used in damp situations, that their switches should be moisture or splashproof. Dimming of lights in poultry houses can be performed by a variable voltage transformer or by an electronic device. This can be an aid to good

Full environmental control for livestock building

husbandry and 'under-running' lamps has the additional advantage of prolonging lamp life. Special controls and fittings are available which allow fluorescent lighting to be dimmed successfully.

VENTILATION AND HEATING CONTROL SYSTEMS FOR LIVESTOCK HOUSES

Sophisticated systems are used in most pig and poultry buildings to control ventilation rates and thereby house temperatures. Some include provision for controlling a heating system in such a way that heat is only used when ventilation is at a minimum, to ensure efficient energy use. Most control panels incorporate automatic fan speed control down to 10% of the fan's maximum speed, or sequential switching of fans, to ensure that the best use is made of the stock's metabolic heat, whether or not additional heat is required. To benefit from these devices, the operator needs to understand how they work and how the best performance from livestock is obtained by correct control setting and careful checking of house temperatures.

The following describes one particular system for control of temperature by varying fan speed.

The panel has two main control knobs. One of these is to set the temperature required in the house. The other sets the minimum speed at which the fan should run to give minimum ventilation (usually 10%). It is important that the installing contractor should check, before he completes an installation, that the minimum speed can in fact be achieved by the fan. (This may be checked using a stroboscope or voltmeter. There have been cases of controllers in livestock buildings claimed to be capable of reducing fan speed to 10% which in fact only reduce to 40% of maximum.)

At installation, the contractor should check the temperature calibration but it will need rechecking at least once a year. This can easily be carried out by the user, using the following method.

Automatic fan speed control

A procedure for checking temperature calibration:

❶ Mount an accurate thermometer close to the sensing element (thermistor or sensor bulb) in the pig or poultry house.

❷ Switch on the fans and set the controller for automatic operation and allow about half an hour to warm up.

❸ Set the minimum speed knob to minimum (usually 10%).

❹ Set the temperature control for a very high temperature (say 30 to 40°C). (The fans should now be running at their slowest speed).

❺ Very slowly rotate knob towards a lower temperature until the noise from the fans indicate that they are running about half way between minimum and full speed.

❻ Note the temperature indicated by the knob pointer when this happens.

❼ Note the actual air temperature on the thermometer near the sensor.

If the readings from steps 6 and 7 are identical ,the controller is accurately calibrated. If there is a significant difference (say more than 5°C) then the manufacturer or installing contractor should be requested to recalibrate the controller.

If the controller is only about 2°C out of calibration, this may be acceptable providing the knob is set to compensate for the error. For example, if the reading for step 6 is 20°C when the actual temperature (step 7) is 18°C, the controller should always be set 2 degrees higher than is required, otherwise the house would be colder than expected.

Note: only a competent electrician should make any connections or adjustments inside a control panel. A layman opening the panel would be exposed to danger and also hazard the future operation of the system.

See *HSE GS30: Health & safety hazards associated with pig husbandry.*

TREATMENT AFTER ELECTRIC SHOCK

If someone receives an electric shock, immediate and speedy action within two to three minutes is essential to minimise the risk of brain damage. The following steps should be taken:

Switch off power
Do this immediately. If you cannot find the switch, shout for help and send someone else to disconnect the electricity.

Free from contact
Remove the casualty from danger: electricity, water, gas, fumes etc. Safeguard yourself when doing so. If the casualty is still in contact with electricity

and the supply cannot be isolated, stand on dry non-conducting material: rubber mat, wood or linoleum. Use rubber gloves, dry clothing, dry rope or wood to pull or push the casualty away from hazard.

 DO NOT ATTEMPT TO REMOVE A PERSON FROM CONTACT AT HIGH VOLTAGE (1000V+)
If contact with high voltage is suspected, telephone your Electricity Company to switch off the supply.

After Release
Do not waste time moving the patient but lay him down on his back, on something dry if possible. If the casualty is not breathing start ventilation at once and send someone else for a doctor and ambulance.

VENTILATION: MOUTH-TO- MOUTH METHOD
This should preferably be learned from a qualified instructor and practised regularly.

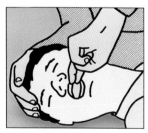

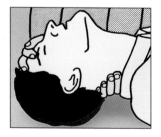

Remove any obstructions to breathing: false teeth, vomit etc, and loosen neckwear.

To open the air passage, tilt the patient's head backwards as far as possible with one hand and with the other, pull his jaw

forward, at the same time slightly opening the patient's mouth.

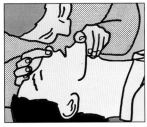

Then pinch the patient's nose shut, take a deep breath, place your mouth over the patient's mouth and blow.

Give 6 to 8 quick blows and continue to inflate the chest about 10 times per minute. Watch the chest during inflation - it should rise.

No movement indicates a blocked airway. If so, check mouth and throat are clear and tilt the head further backwards.

CHECK PULSE

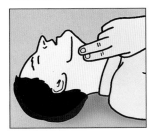

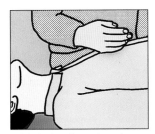

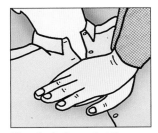

Check the patient's pulse. If it is present, continue inflations until he recovers normal breathing. If no pulse is present, the heart has stopped beating. Lay the patient back on a firm surface, eg the floor.

With the hand cup shaped, strike his chest over the heart position once without follow through weight.
Then if his pulse returns continue with inflations until breathing recovers.

No pulse indicates that the patient's heart is not beating. With the patient lying back on a firm surface, eg the floor, commence external chest compressions and continue mouth-to-mouth ventilation.

One first aider:- 15 chest compressions at 80 per minute, followed by 2 mouth-to-mouth ventilations.

Two first aiders:- One conducts chest compressions without pause at 80 per minute. The other administers mouth-to-mouth ventilation after each 5th chest compression. Check heart beat after first minute and then after every three minutes. Continue external chest compression and mouth-to-mouth ventilation until a normal pulse is felt and colour improves.

Pulse and breathing recover
When normal breathing commences, place the casualty on his side in the recovery position and lightly cover with blankets or similar material. Watch him closely for difficulty in breathing.

OTHER INJURIES
After breathing, priority should be given to controlling bleeding. This is achieved by firm pressure on the wound. Cover with a clean dressing and bandage firmly in place. If bleeding continues add further dressings on top of the first and increase the pressure by bandaging firmly in place. Burns should be covered with a clean, sterile dressing to exclude air. The dressing should be bandaged lightly in position.

Unless it is dangerous to do so, leave the casualty at the site of the accident; expert assistance should be sought before other injuries are treated. If it is necessary to move the casualty, do so with the utmost gentleness carefully supporting any injured parts.

APPENDIX 1

ELECTRICAL TERMINOLOGY

This section is to help the reader understand the meaning of commonly used electrical terms.

Volt (V)

Electrical voltage, pressure (or potential). The mains supply is normally 240V single phase or 415V three phase.

Extra low voltage

Not exceeding 25 volts

Low voltage

Not exceeding 1000 volts, usually 240V or 415V

High voltage

More than 1000 volts, usually 11 000V, 33 000V or higher

Ampere (A)

The rate of flow of current in a circuit.

Watt (W)

Electrical power or load, determined by multiplying the voltage applied to a circuit by the current flow ie V x A = W.

For example a 240V heater carrying a current of 5A is rated at a power of: 240 x 5 = 1200W

Kilowatt (kW)

The kilowatt (1000W) is more commonly used for rating electrical appliances since the watt is a relatively small unit.

Kilowatt hour (kWh)

A unit of electrical energy (one unit of electricity), eg a 1000W (1kW) appliance would use 1 unit (1kWh) of electricity in 1 hour or 2 units (2kWh) of electricity in 2 hours etc.

Horsepower (hp)

746 watts. The output of a machine given in horsepower may be approximately converted into kilowatts(kW) by multiplying by 0.75, eg a 5hp electric motor has a rated power output of 5 x .75 = 3.75kW. (NB owing to internal losses the input to a motor will be slightly greater than its rated output).

Single phase (1Ø)

240V supply system having 3 wires; live,neutral and earth. Used for smaller farms and domestic premises.

Three phase (3Ø)

415/240V supply system having 5 wires; 3 live, one neutral and one earth. Used for larger farms or where large motors are installed. (NB the voltage between live phases is 415V whilst the live phase to neutral voltage is 240V)

Transformer

A device for changing the voltage from one level to another, eg a 240/110V step down transformer.

Capacitor (Condenser)

A device used to assist the starting of some single phase electric motors or to prevent radio interference from electrical equipment.

Bonding

Connection of exposed metalwork to create an equal potential to reduce risk of electric shock (particularly important in livestock buildings including milking parlours, bathrooms etc).

Alternating current (a.c.)

An electric current that reverses direction, ie the voltage and current rise and fall in a sine wave pattern. The number of complete cycles in a second is the frequency of the supply (50 cycles per second is standard in the UK). The mains supply and outputs from generators are a.c. unless rectified to produce direct current.

Direct current (d.c.)

A continuous current that flows in one direction only. The electricity supplied by batteries is d.c. and rectifiers will convert alternating currents to d.c..

APPENDIX 2
LEGISLATION AND STANDARDS

STATUTORY REFERENCES

Some of the important statutory documents are:

▲ Agricultural (Safety, Health and Welfare Provisions) Act 1956

▲ Agriculture (Stationary Machinery) Regulations 1959

▲ Factories Act 1961

▲ Health and Safety at Work etc. Act 1974

▲ Electricity at Work Regulations 1989 - Memorandum of guidance HS(R)25

NON-STATUTORY REFERENCES

The following references may be helpful in determining acceptable safe standards for electrical apparatus and equipment:

IEE Wiring Regulations (Regulations for electrical installations)

BRITISH STANDARDS:

▲ BS 2769 Portable electric motor operated tools.

▲ BS 4343 Industrial plugs, socket-outlets and couplers for a.c. and d.c. supplies.

▲ BS 196 Protected-type, non-reversible plugs, socket-outlets, cable-couplers and appliance-couplers with earthing contacts for single phase a.c. circuits up to 250V.

▲ BS 1363 13 amp plugs, switched and unswitched socket-outlets and boxes.

▲ BS 3006 Industrial plugs and socket outlets and couplers for a.c. and d.c. supplies.

▲ BS 5502 Code of Practice for the design of buildings and structures for agriculture.

▲ BS 2632 Mains-operated electric fence controllers.

▲ BS 6167 Battery operated electric fence controllers not suitable for connection to the supply mains.

▲ BS 6369 Battery operated electric fence controllers suitable for connection to the supply mains.

▲ BS 4533 Section 102.8.1982 Luminaires - specification for handlamps.

Health and Safety Executive Guidance Notes

▲ *GS6 Avoidance of danger from overhead electric lines*

▲ *GS53 Avoiding danger from buried electricity lines*

▲ *GS37 Flexible leads, plugs and sockets etc.*

▲ *GS27 Protection against electric shock*

▲ *PM32 Safe use of portable electrical apparatus*

▲ *PM29 Electrical hazards from steam/water pressure cleaners etc.*

▲ *PM38 Selection and use of electric handlamps.*

▲ *PM64 Electrical safety in arc welding*

▲ *PM53 Emergency private generation: electrical safety*

OTHER REFERENCES

▲ *The Safe Use of Irrigation Equipment near Overhead Electric Power Lines* (Electricity Association) available from Electricity Companies

▲ *Recommendations on the Avoidance of Danger from Underground Electricity Cables* (National Joint Utilities Group) pocket card available from Electricity Companies

▲ *Farm Electric Handbook Essentials of Farm Lighting* Electricity Association

▲ *Bulletin 147 Electric Fencing* MAFF

▲ *General Lighting Layouts for Farm Buildings* (Technical Information Sheet AGR 5-2) Electricity Association

▲ *HS(G)47 Avoiding danger from underground services* Health and Safety Executive

▲ *Preventing accidents to children in agriculture* Health and Safety Executive

APPENDIX 3

RELEVANT NPTC AND SAYFC TESTS

Test items relating to the use of electricity and/or electrical installations occur in the following proficiency tests.

National Proficiency Tests Council tests:

Milk production

Beef production

Sheep production

Pig production

Mechanised operations

Poultry production - broilers/capons

Poultry production - ducks

Poultry production - egg production

Poultry production - hatchery practice

Poultry production - turkeys

Farm maintenance

Scottish Association of Young Farmers Clubs tests:

Welding (electric arc)

Machine milking

Sheep shearing

Cattle dressing (dairy)

Cattle dressing (beef)

Barn machinery test

APPENDIX 4

HOW TO READ YOUR ELECTRICITY METER

It makes good sense to read your meter regularly to keep a check on your electricity consumption. A meter is easy to read if the advice given below is followed.

DIAL 1 Pointer has passed 4, reading is 4

DIAL 2 Pointer is over 5 but reading is 4 in this case

DIAL 3 Pointer has passed 9, reading is 9

DIAL 4 Pointer has passed 2, reading is 2

DIAL 5 Pointer is directly over 8, reading is 8 in this case

Ignore this dial

The correct dial reading is 44928

The 'readout' display on electricity meters uses a number of dials or a digital 'window'.

Since the introduction of day/night tariffs, digital meters have been manufactured with two displays - the top one marked 'low' and the bottom one 'normal'. An arrow tells you which display is engaged and a time switch controls the arrow according to the time of day.

LOW 0 1 2 3 4 2

kWh

NORMAL 0 0 3 5 5 1

Digital two rate meter

When reading your dial meter, always remember that adjacent dials revolve in opposite directions. Ignore the dial marked 1/10(it's only there for testing purposes) and read the other five dials from left to right.

Points to Note

a. If the pointer is approximately central between two numbers (say 4 and 5) write down the lower number.

b. If the pointer is close to a number (say 5), look at the dial to the right to see if it is pointing at a high figure (say 7-9) or at a low figure (say 1-3).

c. If a high figure (dial 3) then write down 4 (dial 2) because it has not quite reached 5 yet.

d. If a low figure, then write down 5 because it would have just passed 5.

Digital type meters are very simple to read because the reading is indicated in figures rather like the mileometer in a car.

With both the dial meter and the digital meter, when you've worked out the reading, subtract the previous reading shown on your bill to find the number of units of electricity used.

Digital three rate meter

APPENDIX 5

USEFUL ADDRESSES

The electricity industry operates a nationwide service for farmers and growers. This service is available through your Electricity Company and is backed by the information and demonstration facilities of the Farm Electric Centre, situated at the National Agricultural Centre, Stoneleigh, Kenilworth, Warwickshire. CV8 2LS. Telephone: Coventry (0203) 696512 Fax: (0203) 696360

Whenever you want facts, information or advice about the uses of electricity in farming or horticulture, your Electricity Company's agricultural engineer will be pleased to help.

Electricity's agricultural staff help farmers become energy efficient

ELECTRICITY COMPANY HEADQUARTERS

East Midlands Electricity plc
PO Box 4 North PDO
398 Coppice Road
Arnold, Nottingham
NG5 7HX
Tel: Nottingham (0602) 269711

Eastern Electricity plc
PO Box 40
Wherstead
Ipswich
Suffolk
IP9 2AQ
Tel: Ipswich (0473) 688688

London Electricity plc
Templar House
81-87 High Holborn
London
WC1V 6NU
Tel: 071-242 9050

MANWEB plc
Sealand Road
Chester
CH1 4LR
Tel: Chester (0244) 377111

Midlands Electricity plc
Mucklow Hill
Halesowen
West Midlands
B62 8BP
Tel: 021-423 2345

Northern Electric plc
Carliol House
Market Street
Newcastle-Upon-Tyne
NE1 6NE
Tel: 091-221 2000

NORWEB plc
Talbot Road
Manchester
M16 0HQ
Tel: 061-873 8000

Scottish Hydro-Electric plc
16 Rothesay Terrace
Edinburgh
EH3 7SE
Tel: 031-225 1361

Scottish Power plc
Cathcart House
Spean Street
Glasgow
G44 4BE
Tel: 041-637 7177

SEEBOARD plc
Grand Avenue
Hove
East Sussex
BN3 2LS
Tel: Brighton (0273) 724522

South Wales Electricity plc
St Mellons
Cardiff
CF3 9XW
Tel: Cardiff (0222) 792111

South Western Electricity plc
800 Park Avenue
Aztec West
Almondsbury
Bristol BS12 4SE
Tel: Almondsbury (0454) 201101

Southern Electric plc
Littlewick Green
Nr Maidenhead
Berkshire
SL6 3QB
Tel: Littlewick Green
(0628) 822166

Yorkshire Electricity Group plc
Wetherby Road
Scarcroft
Leeds
LS14 3HS
Tel: Leeds (0532) 892123

The National Grid Company plc
National Grid House
Sumner Street
London
SE1 9JU
Tel: 071-620 8000

National Power PLC
Senator House
85 Queen Victoria Street
London
EC4V 4DP
Tel: 071-454 9494

PowerGen plc
Haslucks Green Road
Shirley
Solihull
West Midlands
B90 4PD
Tel: 021-701 2000

Northern Ireland Electricity
120 Malone Road
Belfast
BT9 5HT
Tel: Belfast (0232) 661100

Manx Electricity Authority
PO Box 177
Victoria Road
Douglas
Isle of Man
Tel: (0624) 625811

The Jersey Electricity Company Limited
PO Box 45,
Queens Road
St. Helier,
Jersey C.I.
Tel: (0534) 505000

States of Guernsey Electricity Board
PO Box 4
Electricity House
North Side
Vale, Guernsey C.I.
Tel: (0481) 46931

Electricity Supply Board
27 Lower Fitzwilliam Street
Dublin 2
Eire
Tel: Dublin 765831

Nuclear Electric PLC
Barnett Way
Barnwood
Gloucester
GL4 7RS
Tel: (0452) 652222

Scottish Nuclear Limited
Minto Building
6 Inverlair Avenue
Glasgow
G44 4AD
Tel: 041-633 1166

ACKNOWLEDGEMENTS

The Farm Electric Centre wishes to thank the following who assisted in the preparation of this publication.

Andrew Sykes Limited

Agricultural Training Board

Association of Agricultural Educational Staffs

Electrical Contractors' Association

Electricity Association-
Engineering & Safety Division, Safety Group

Health and Safety Executive

H.M. Agricultural Inspectorate

Massey-Ferguson (UK) Ltd.

National Farmers Union, England and Wales

National Farmers Union, Scotland

The National Grid Company plc

National Inspection Council for Electrical Installation Contracting

National Proficiency Tests Council

National Union of Agricultural and Allied Workers

Simmonds Brothers

The Royal Agricultural Society of England

Warwickshire College of Agriculture

Designed in England by Bruce, Davis Associates, Design Consultants